This badass coloring book belongs to:

. . . .

This is a booklet for when you feel overwhelmed.
And life tends to be quite overwhelming.

Coloring can help you quiet the mind. The words on each page
can help you open the heart.

This also works well when dealing with anxiety,
because it distracts the mind from overthinking
and the anxious body impulse is channeled through
the pencil and translated onto paper.

Powerful stuff this can be, I tell you.

Use one color only or feel free to experiment.

If you want to see what the puzzles are, check the last page.

If you want to enjoy the discovery, start coloring right away.

A spiroglyphic is a spiral puzzle, you color inside the line, and
it varies in width as it winds towards the centre.

The simplest way to fill one in is to start
at an end of the spiral and just color towards the middle.

Pause to see if you can discern what the image is,
then work out along the spiral to the edge again,
to reveal the image.

For different effects, color with different shades,
or divide the spiroglyphic into sections, coloring each differently.

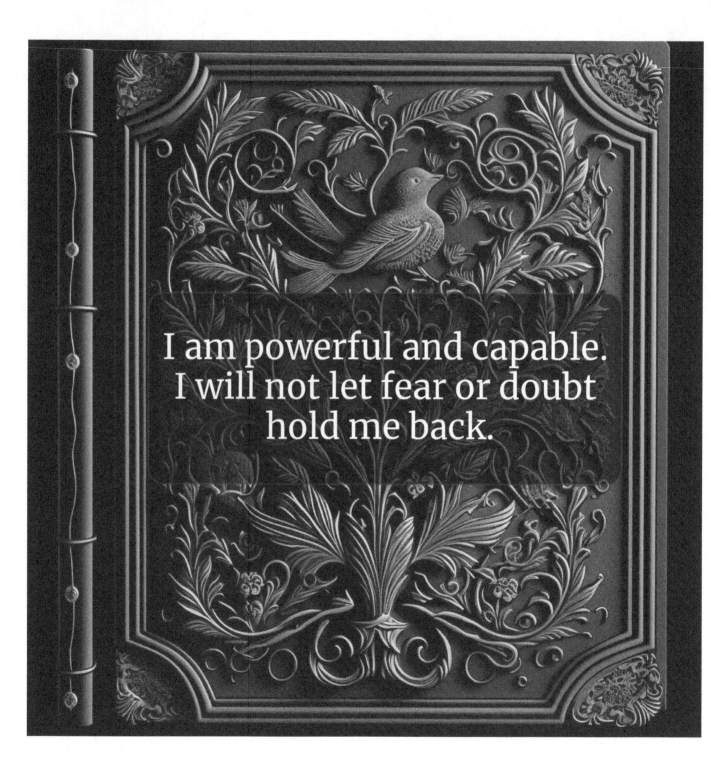

I am powerful and capable.
I will not let fear or doubt
hold me back.

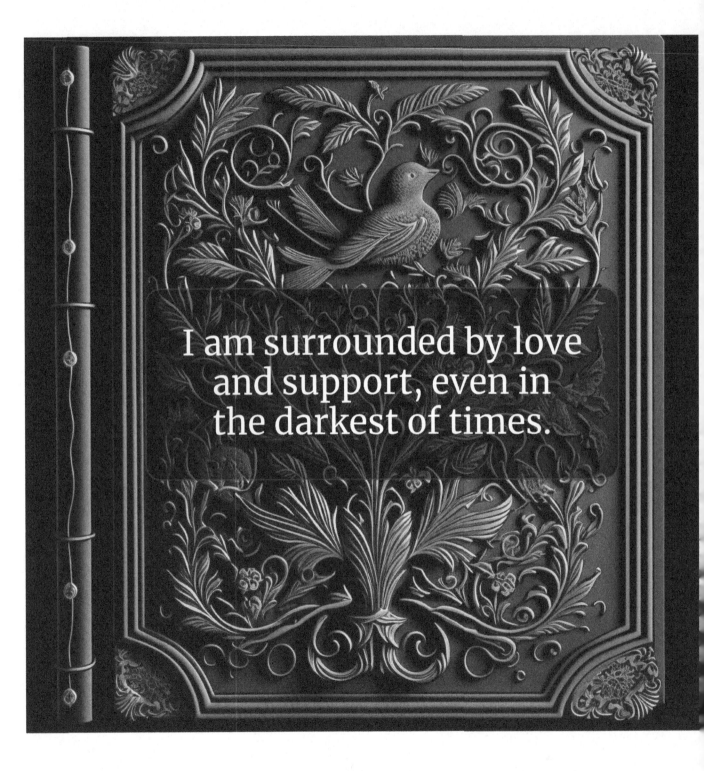

I am surrounded by love
and support, even in
the darkest of times.

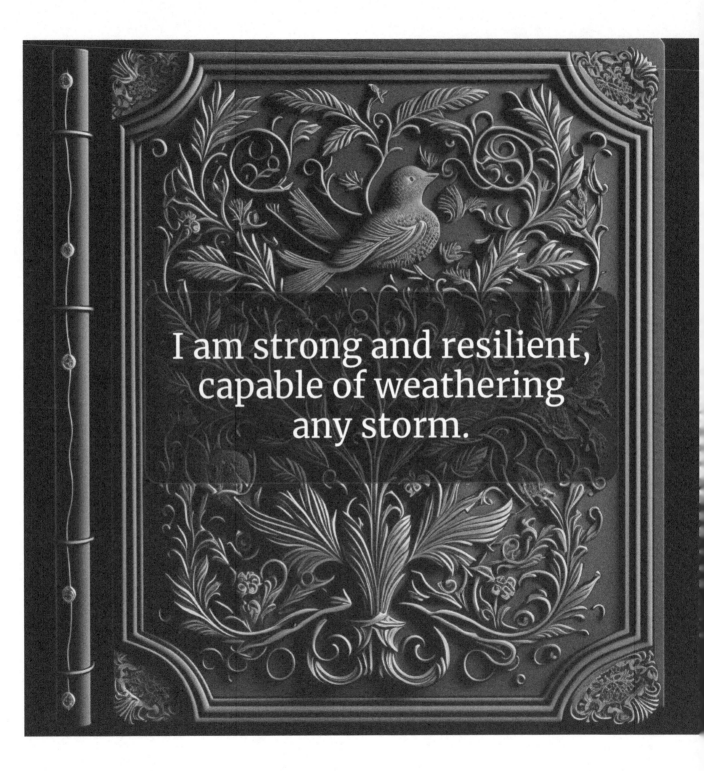

I am strong and resilient,
capable of weathering
any storm.

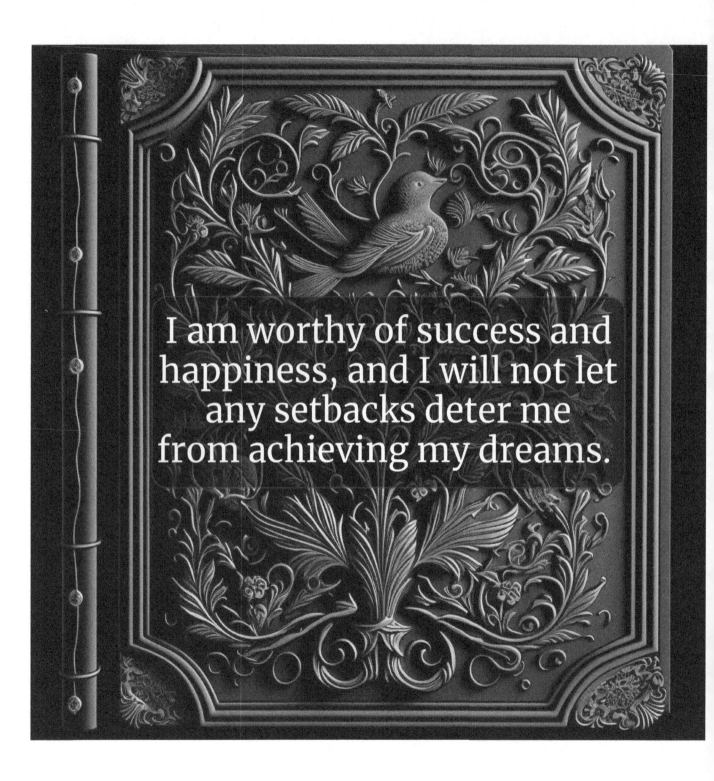

I am worthy of success and happiness, and I will not let any setbacks deter me from achieving my dreams.

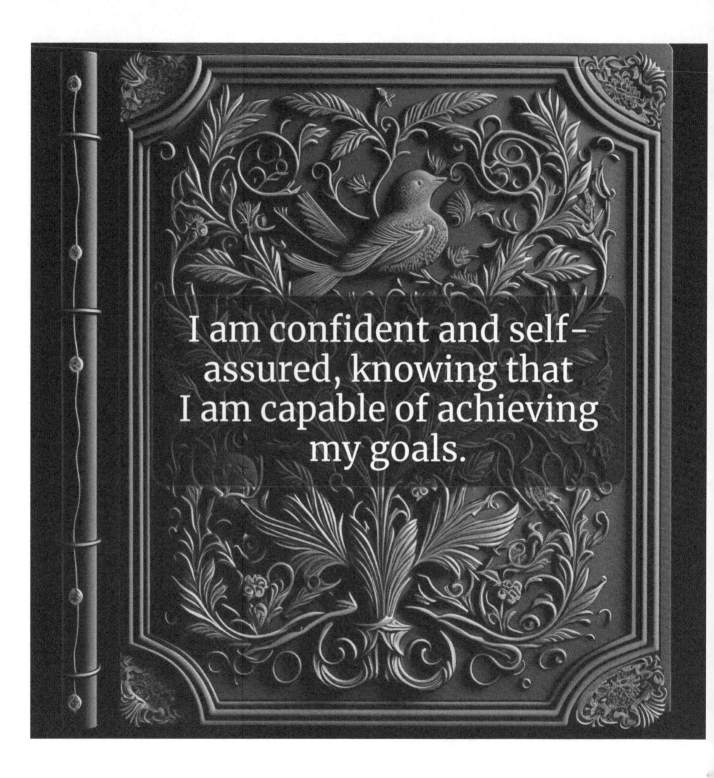

I am confident and self-assured, knowing that I am capable of achieving my goals.

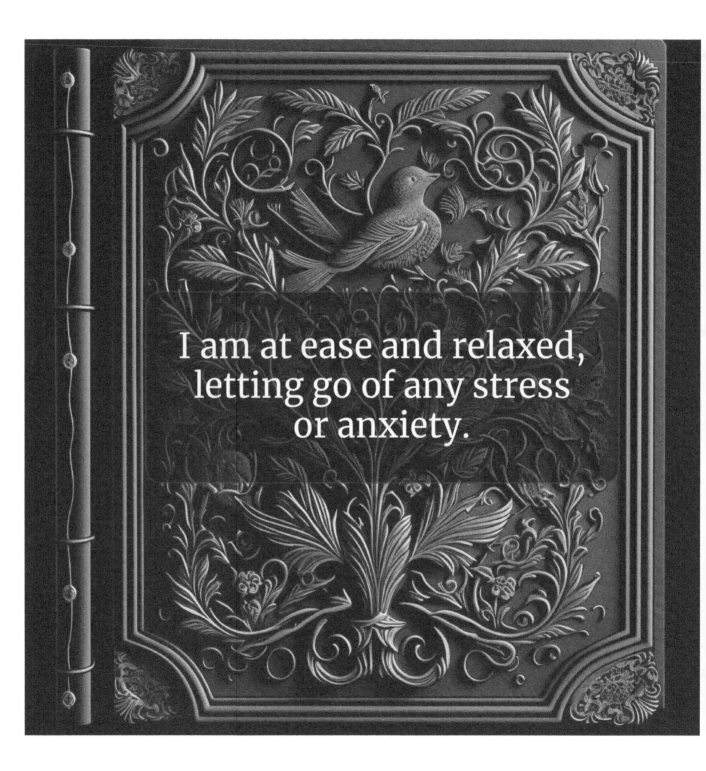

I am at ease and relaxed, letting go of any stress or anxiety.

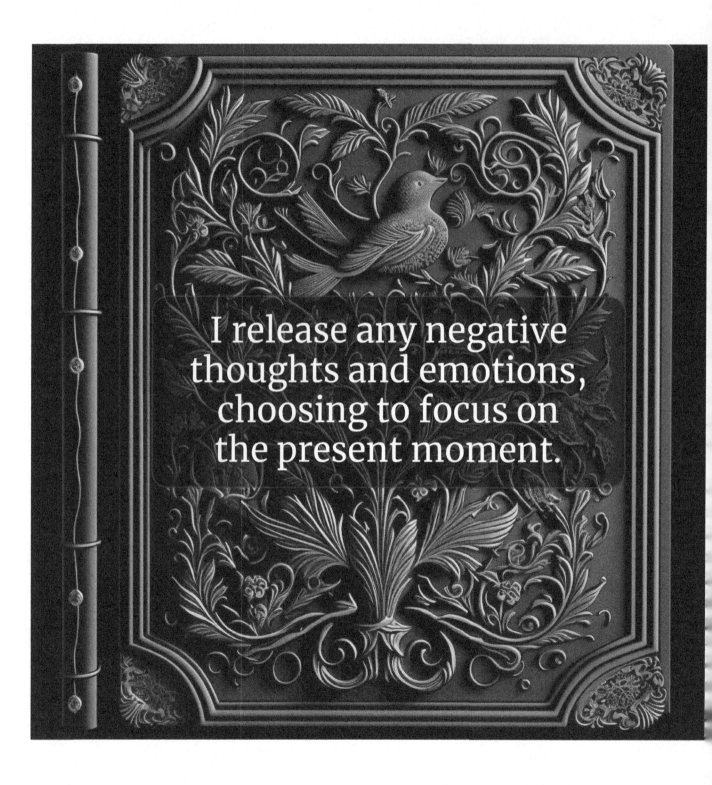

I release any negative thoughts and emotions, choosing to focus on the present moment.

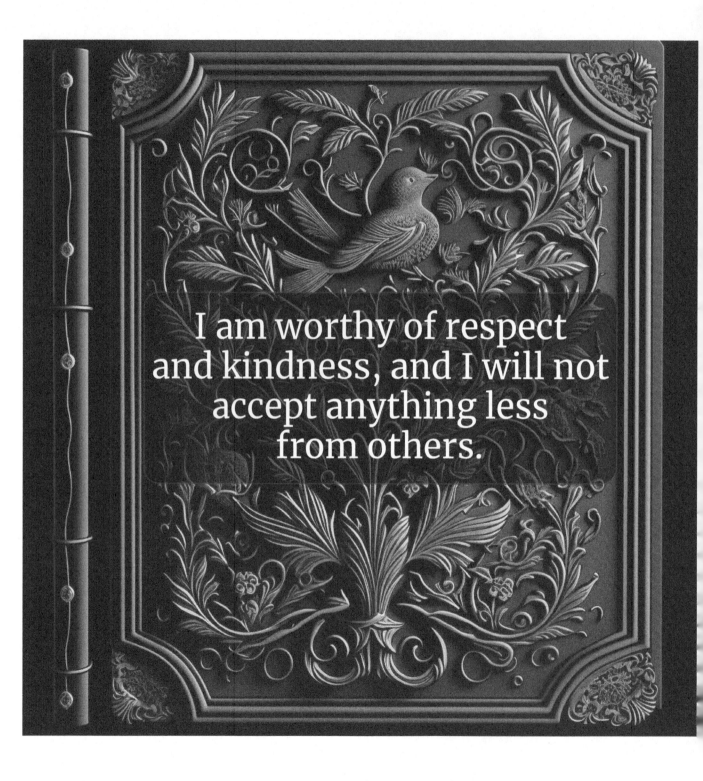

I am worthy of respect and kindness, and I will not accept anything less from others.

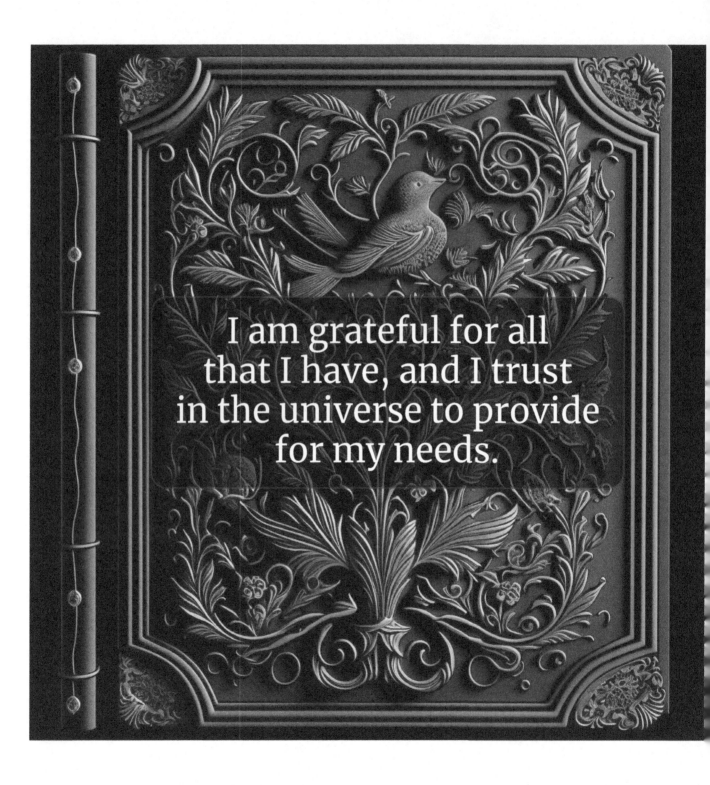

I am grateful for all that I have, and I trust in the universe to provide for my needs.

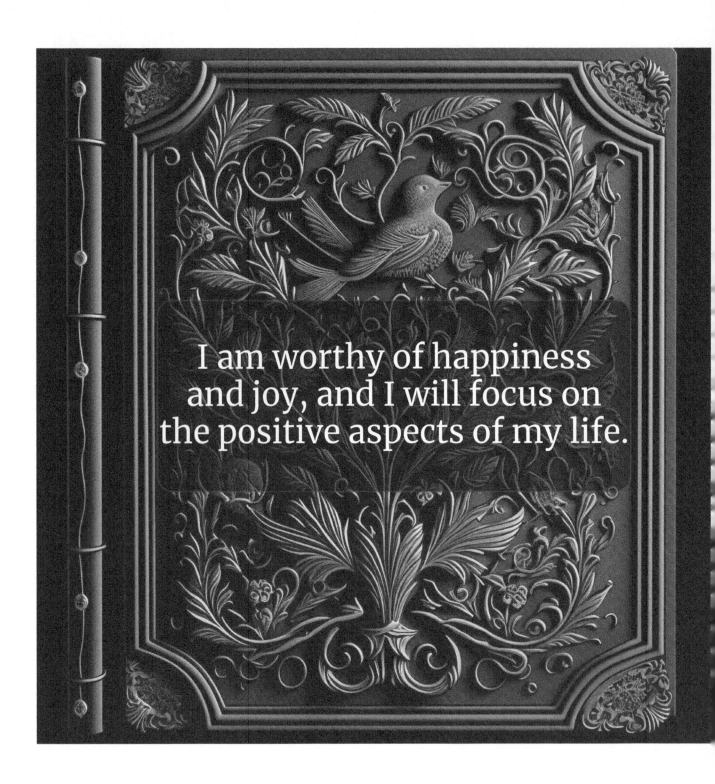

I am worthy of happiness and joy, and I will focus on the positive aspects of my life.

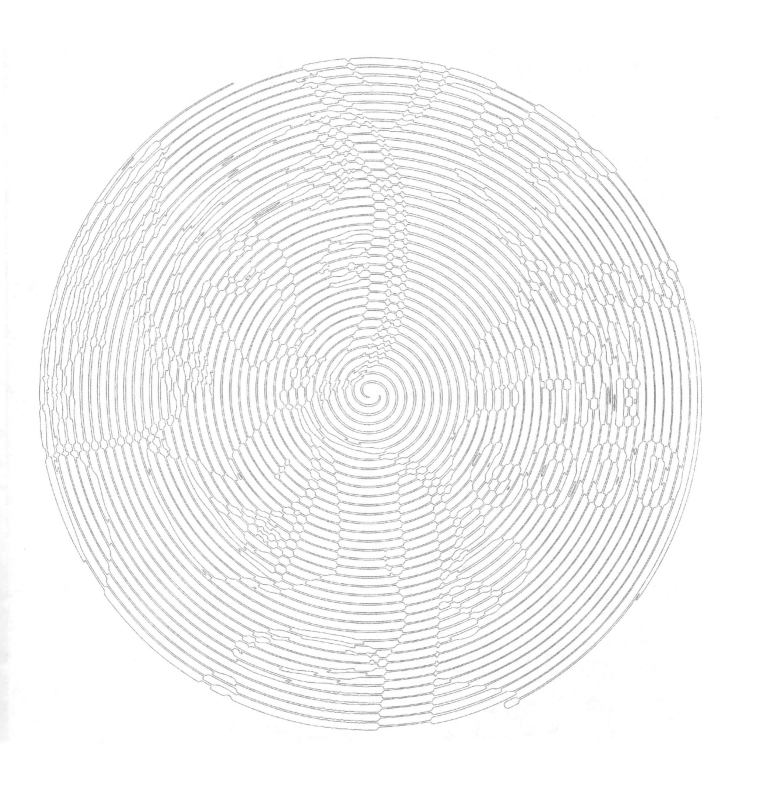

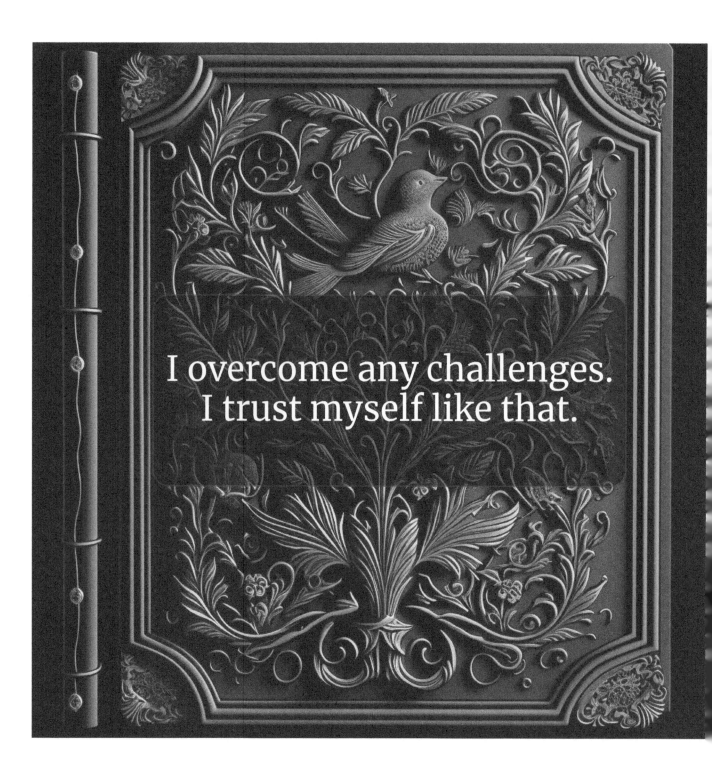

I overcome any challenges.
I trust myself like that.

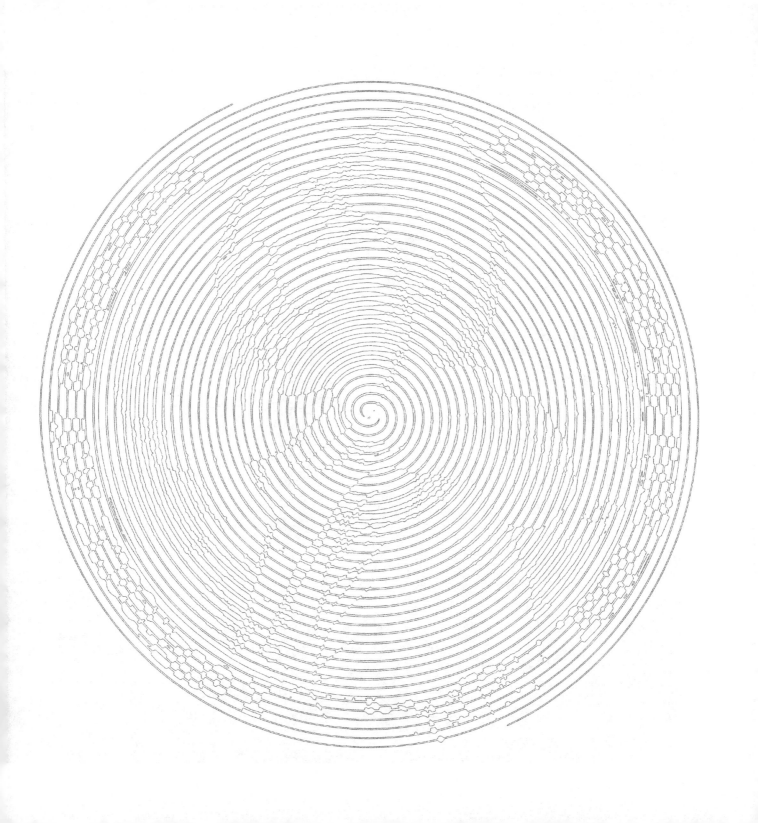

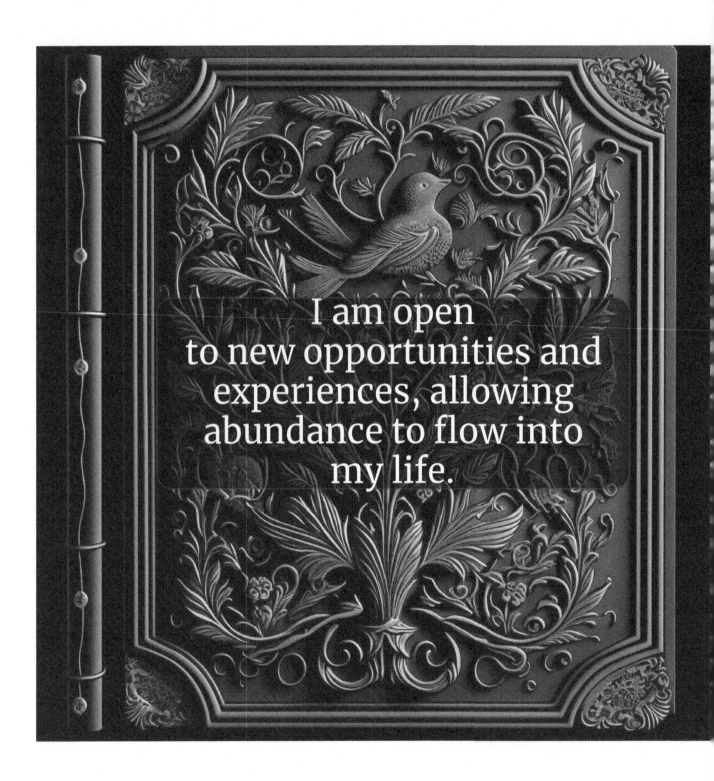

I am open
to new opportunities and
experiences, allowing
abundance to flow into
my life.

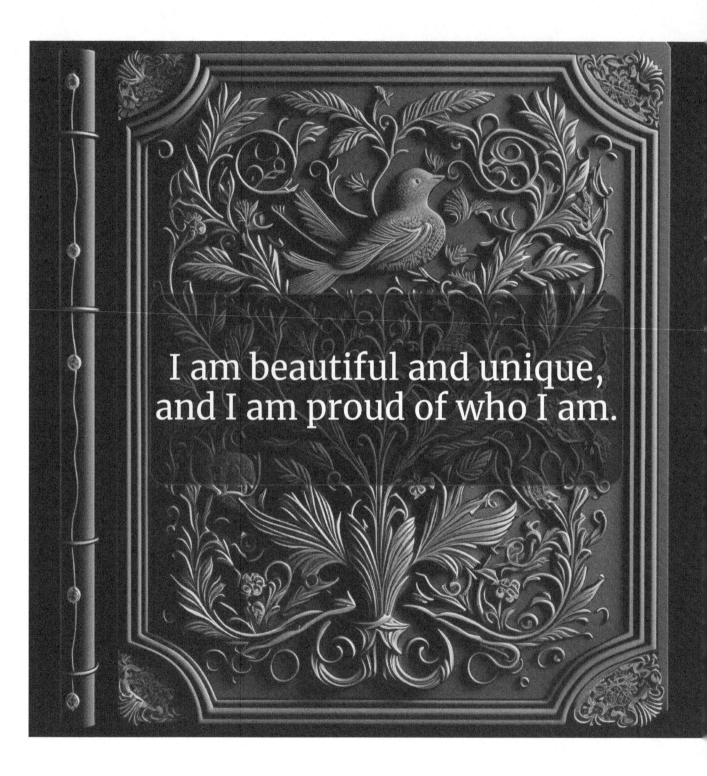

I am beautiful and unique, and I am proud of who I am.

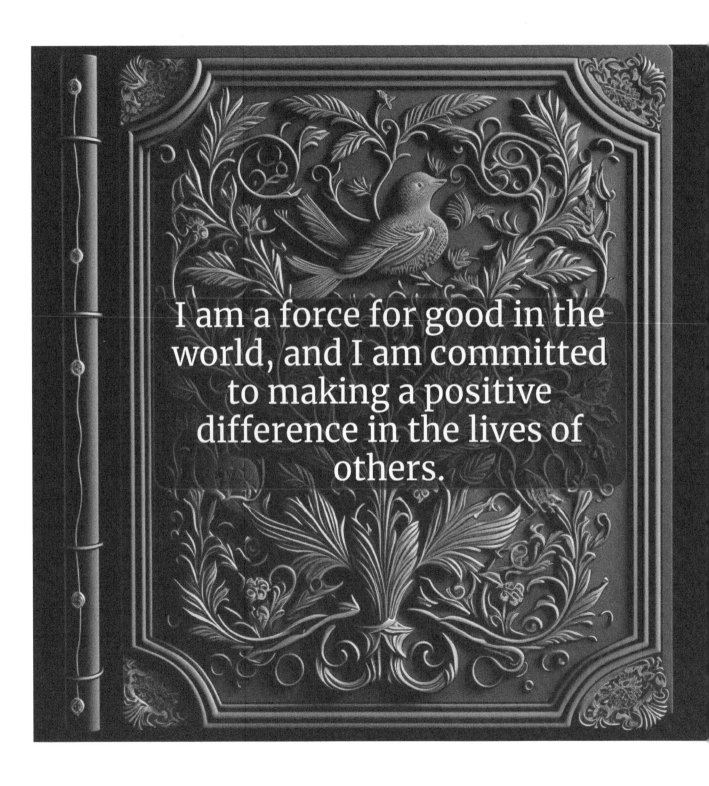

I am a force for good in the world, and I am committed to making a positive difference in the lives of others.

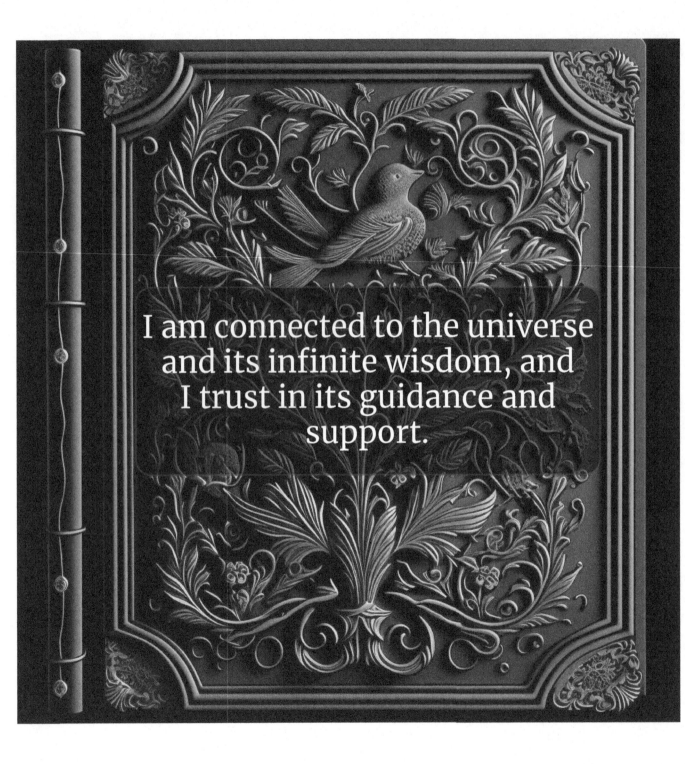

I am connected to the universe and its infinite wisdom, and I trust in its guidance and support.

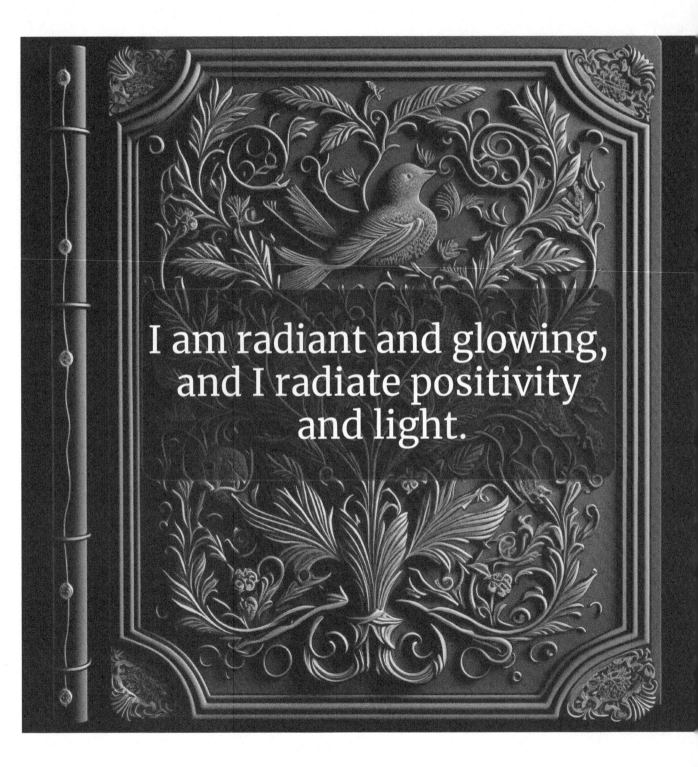

I am radiant and glowing, and I radiate positivity and light.

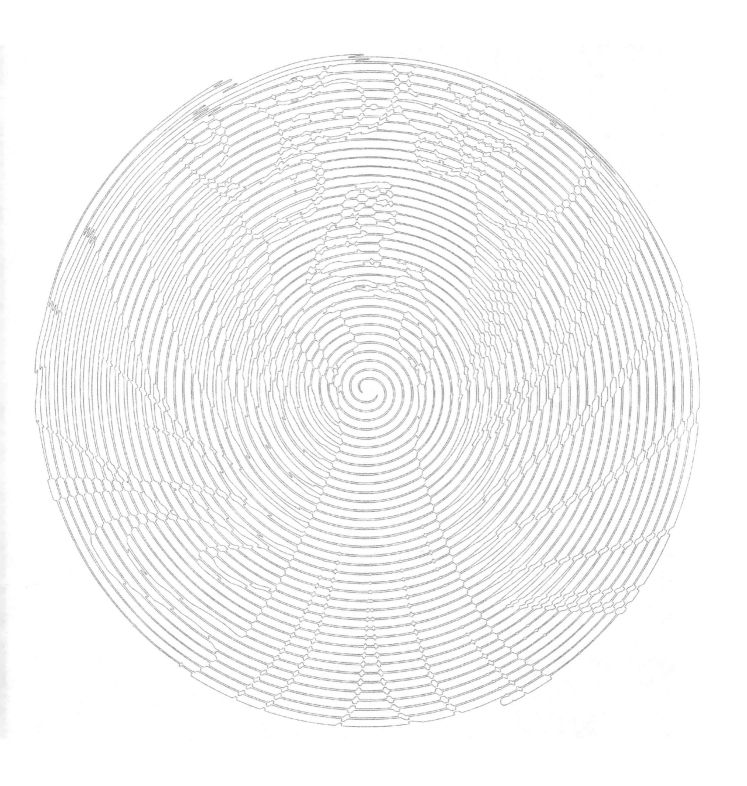

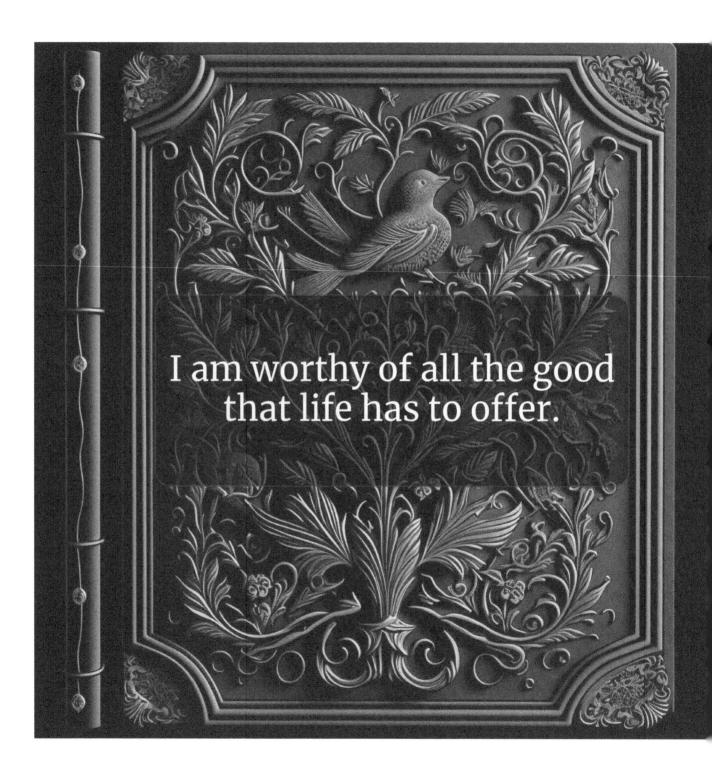

I am worthy of all the good that life has to offer.

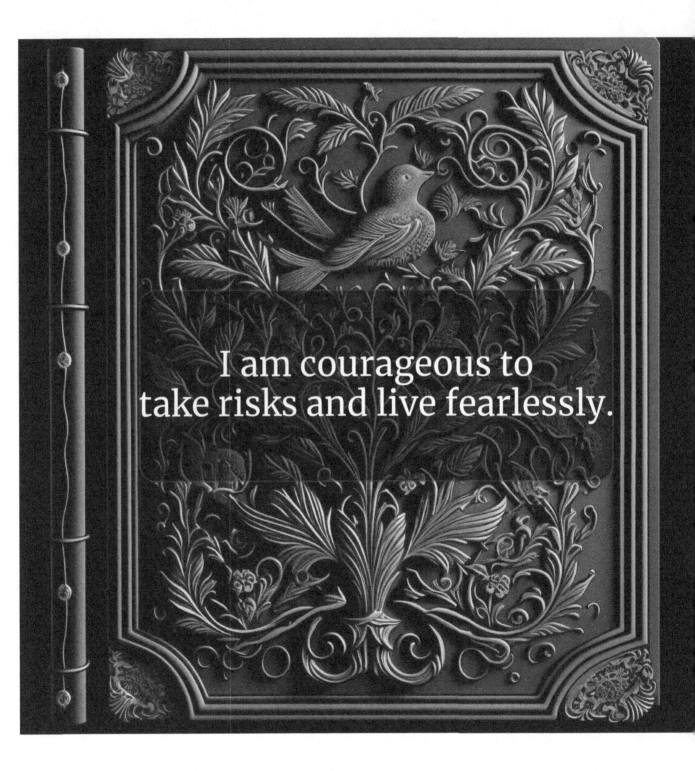

I am courageous to
take risks and live fearlessly.

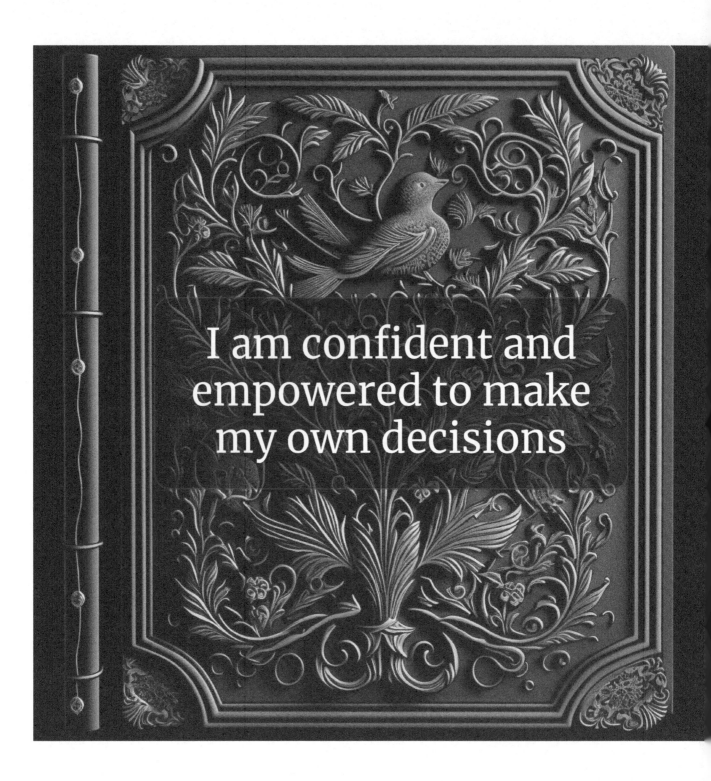

I am confident and empowered to make my own decisions

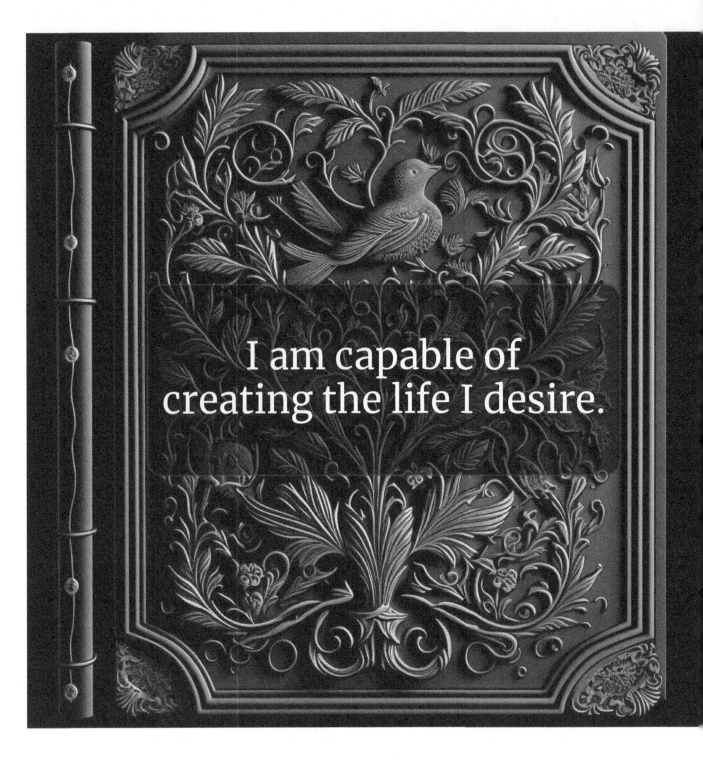

I am capable of creating the life I desire.

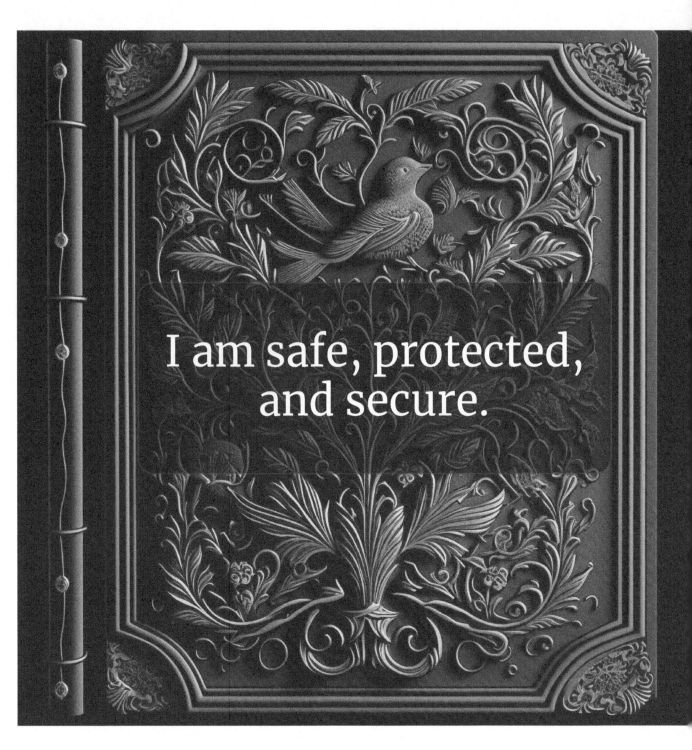

I am safe, protected, and secure.

Made in the USA
Las Vegas, NV
15 December 2023

82898181R00033